P9-DHK-123

WHAT'S THE BIG IDEA?

SOCIETY
AND SOCIAL
ORGANIZATION

Tim Cooke

Cavendish
Square

New York

Published in 2018 by Cavendish Square Publishing, LLC
243 5th Avenue, Suite 136 New York, NY 10016

© 2018 Brown Bear Books Ltd

Website: cavendishsq.com

This publication represents the opinions and views of the author based on his or her personal experiences, knowledge, and research. The information in this book serves as a general guide only. The author and publisher have used their best efforts in preparing this book and disclaim liabilty rising directly or indirectly for the use and application of this book.

CPSIA compliance information: Batch #CS17CSQ:

All websites were available and accurate when this book went to press.

Library of Congress Cataloging-in-Publication Data

Names: Cooke, Tim.
Title: Society and social organization / Tim Cooke.
Description: New York : Cavendish Square, 2018. | Series: What's the big idea? | Includes index.
Identifiers: ISBN 9781502628220 (library bound) | ISBN 9781502628237 (ebook)
Subjects: LCSH: Social systems. | Sociology. | Civil society.
Classification: LCC HM701.C66 2018 | DDC 306.3'6--dc23

For Brown Bear Books Ltd:
Managing Editor: Tim Cooke
Editorial Director: Lindsey Lowe
Designer: Supriya Sahai
Design Manager: Keith Davis
Children's Publisher: Anne O'Daly
Picture Manager: Sophie Mortimer

Picture Credits:
Front Cover: View Apart/Shutterstock.com
Interior: 123rf: 6-7; **Alamy:** Richard Baker News 40, Worldwide Picture Library 9; **Dreamstime:** Nikolay Dimitrov 16, Cristiano Fronteddu 30-31, Amanda Lewis 20, Dmitry Rukhlenko 17, Konstantin Shaklein 27; **Library of Congress:** 28, 33, 34; **Mary Evans Picture Library:** 39; **Public Domain:** Ashmolean Museum 18-19, Bodleian Library 24-25, British Library 26, Detroit Institute of Arts 4, Louvre Museum 21, Margaret Thatcher Foundation 8, UNESCO.org 35, United States Capitol 36-37; **Shutterstock:** 5, 10, 12-13, 15, 22, Eddy Galeotti 32, Everett Historical 38, Scott McGill 11; **Thinkstock:** Peter Denis 23, istockphoto 29, 41.

All other photos artwork and maps, Brown Bear Books.

Brown Bear Books has made every attempt to contact the copyright holder.
If you have any information please contact licensing@brownbearbooks.co.uk

All rights reserved. No part of this book may be reproduced, stored in a retrieval system, or transmitted in any form or by any means, electronic, mechanical, photocopying, recording, or otherwise, without the prior written permission of the copyright holder.

Manufactured in the United States of America

CONTENTS

INTRODUCTION

Most people today accept that they live in a society. However, throughout history people have tried to define what society is and how individuals fit within it.

A society is everyone who lives in the same place and who belongs to the same system of cultural, social, and economic relationships, or lives under the same political system. Although defining this idea seems simple, society is complex. A family is a type of society, but so is a neighborhood, a city, a country—or even a whole area of the world, such as when people talk about "Western society." A person has different relationships with different types of societies.

In the 1500s the artist Pieter Brueghel the Elder painted many scenes of peasant life. It was the first time ordinary people had been represented as distinct individuals.

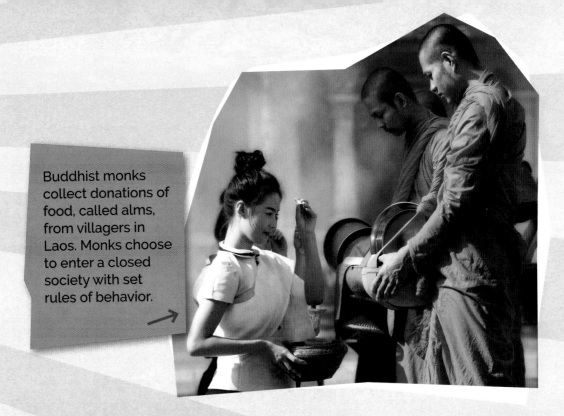

Buddhist monks collect donations of food, called alms, from villagers in Laos. Monks choose to enter a closed society with set rules of behavior.

Within any society, there are smaller societies. For example, a high school is a society, within which there may be a science club or a sports club. Each type of smaller society has its own rules.

Another aspect of the idea of society is the inclusion of outsiders. Nearly all societies—apart from those such as clubs that people choose to join—also include people who do not want to be included. These people may reject the society's rules, or feel that they have nothing in common with other members of the society.

Difficult questions

Outsiders raise questions about the relationship between a society and individuals. Does a society have the right to impose its values on all its members? Since the late 1940s, it has been generally recognized that people have rights as individuals and not just as members of society. In the past, however, this was not always the case. Individuals were less important than their overall society.

WHAT IS SOCIETY?

The simplest definition of society is a group of people living together in an organized way.

Since before **Neolithic** times, people have lived in groups. However, the **concept** of society is a complex idea. On the one hand, society includes all **interactions** between individuals. Therefore, everyone is a member of society at all times—even those who are **antisocial** or reject the accepted rules of society.

INCLUSIVE

One definition of society is that it includes everyone, no matter who they are.

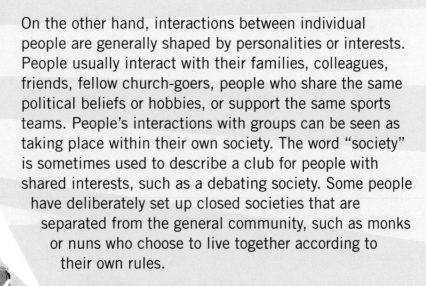

On the other hand, interactions between individual people are generally shaped by personalities or interests. People usually interact with their families, colleagues, friends, fellow church-goers, people who share the same political beliefs or hobbies, or support the same sports teams. People's interactions with groups can be seen as taking place within their own society. The word "society" is sometimes used to describe a club for people with shared interests, such as a debating society. Some people have deliberately set up closed societies that are separated from the general community, such as monks or nuns who choose to live together according to their own rules.

Finding a definition

If society can mean so many things, it is hard to find a single definition. One definition is to say that society includes all people and everything they do. However, this is so broad that it does not really mean anything.

TIMELINE

ca. 30,000 BCE — Early humans begin to paint the walls of caves with images of animals, people, and the shapes of their own hands.

ca. 7500 BCE — Catal Huyuk is settled in what is now Anatolia. It is the oldest known settlement in the world. It was made possible by advances in agriculture.

1987 — British prime minister Margaret Thatcher declares in an interview that "there is no such thing as society."

7

Another definition was proposed in the mid-1800s by the German philosopher Karl Marx. Marx suggested that society is a group of people who are part of a network of economic exchanges. He was influenced by the expansion of industry in the 1700s and 1800s. In Marx's view, members of society produce, sell, or buy goods, so they all have roles as either producers, consumers, workers, or owners. In the 1980s, the British prime minister Margaret Thatcher rejected the suggestion that society had any importance. She argued that the idea of society was no longer useful, declaring that society does not exist.

Origins of society

Society emerged long before modern humans evolved. Many animals cooperate as groups in order to hunt or to raise their young. The earliest humans must have cooperated in similar ways. They lived in a harsh environment in which natural forces and wild animals were a constant threat. Perhaps they began to cooperate as families to hunt animals, then began to work in larger groups. These societies were known as **hunter-gatherers**.

THATCHER

When Margaret Thatcher declared in 1987 that "there is no such thing as society," she was making the point that an all-inclusive definition of society was meaningless.

→

AMAZONIA

Hunter-gatherer women with baskets cross a fallen tree in Amazonia as they set out to collect nuts, berries, and edible leaves and roots.

→

A few small groups of hunter-gatherers still live in remote regions of the world such as Amazonia in South America and New Guinea in Southeast Asia. Experts who study these groups note that they often divide roles based on gender. Men hunt animals, for example, while women gather berries, nuts, and other plants and look after the children. The earliest human societies may have been arranged in a similar way.

TIMELINE OF HUMAN SETTLEMENT

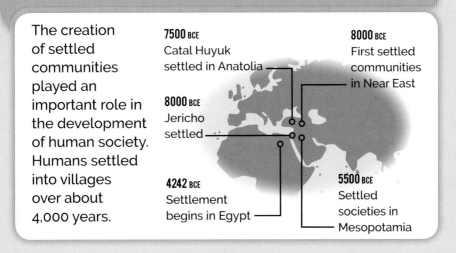

The creation of settled communities played an important role in the development of human society. Humans settled into villages over about 4,000 years.

7500 BCE
Catal Huyuk settled in Anatolia

8000 BCE
First settled communities in Near East

8000 BCE
Jericho settled

4242 BCE
Settlement begins in Egypt

5500 BCE
Settled societies in Mesopotamia

Developing societies

As humans evolved, they developed language and learned to create fire. They also learned how to make tools by chipping rocks into sharp blades. Already some people were taking on special roles within the community.

As early as 30,000 years ago, artists painted people and animals on the walls of caves in Europe, Africa, and Asia. Grinding up natural substances to make colors and then creating the painting must have taken a lot of time. Experts believe people thought that painting the animals was a kind of magical process. It might make the gods send them animals to hunt. Some individuals were probably thought to have a closer relationship with the spirit world than others. These people were the forerunners of priests.

SIMEIZ CAVE

This prehistoric painting was found in a cave in Crimea, Russia. It shows hunters on foot chasing animals, including deer.

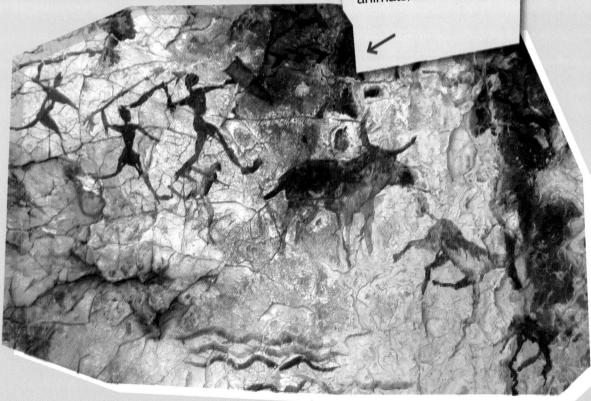

Different roles

As human society developed, individuals must have decided who would do different types of work. They must have figured out who would go hunting and how to share food. The first leaders may have been chosen because they were the strongest or smartest members of a group. As society became more advanced, so were the ways it had to be organized.

SET ROLES

Early people developed specialized roles depending on their skills. Some became craftspeople, making objects such as these arrowheads. Others emerged as rulers, hunters, warriors, and artists.

IN SUMMARY

■ As humans evolved, people learned to live together in societies where they cooperated to benefit the whole group.

■ **Archaeological** evidence such as cave paintings and tools suggest that members of societies soon began to develop specialized roles.

SOCIETY IN THE ANCIENT WORLD

The development of specialized roles within society led to the emergence of early civilizations in the Middle East, the Mediterranean, and Asia.

Around 10,000 years ago, humans learned how to grow plants such as cereals that would produce grains to turn into food. Over centuries, farmers gradually learned to grow a wider variety of crops and to raise **domesticated** animals, such as cows, goats, sheep, and pigs.

THEATER

This Greek theater, built in what is now Turkey in 155 CE, could seat 12,000 people. People from all **classes** of Greek society went to the theater. →

The farming revolution

The advent of farming revolutionized society. Instead of having to move around in search of animals to hunt or food to gather, people could live in settled communities and grow their own food. They produced more food than they needed themselves. This **surplus** meant that not everyone had to be involved in food production—there was enough food to go around. People began to do a wider range of work. Some became priests, others made pottery or learned to work with metal. Some made clothes. People began to exchange goods and skills. They swapped food for cloth, for example. This process is known as **barter**.

Now that society had an economic system, people began to be distinguished from one another by their possessions. Some people owned more things than other people. They could barter more goods to increase their possessions.

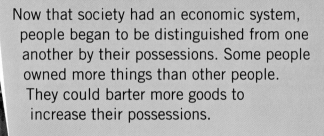

TIMELINE

ca. 8000 BCE Humans begin to learn to grow crops, which gradually leads to the emergence of settled communities.

ca. 3500 BCE Civilizations develop around the world, with large cities, extensive trade, social **hierarchies**, and wide differences between the rich and the poor.

ca. 1500 BCE A **caste system** begins to emerge when a people known as the Aryans arrive in what is now India.

As early as 7,000 years ago, society divided into different classes. Archaeologists have uncovered evidence in tombs that shows that some farmers had better tools than others. Their land may have been more productive than that of their neighbors. Archaeologists have also found evidence that these families passed land from one generation to the next. Those with the best land became wealthy. The seeds of social inequality had been sown.

Wealth and power

Wealth meant that a few people could afford to live luxuriously and work less hard than others. The creation of different levels of wealth in society led to the emergence of privilege and also political power. The wealthiest people began to make decisions that affected the whole group. They used their wealth to reward people who supported them. They became so powerful that they ruled their society as chiefs or kings.

FARMERS

The wealth of ancient Egypt was based on agriculture. Surplus food allowed some people to do jobs that were not directly connected with the land, such as tax collecting (*front, left*).

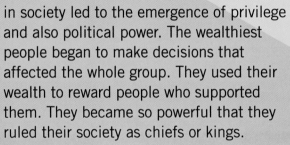

PRIESTS

Priests like these Egyptian priests belonged to the upper levels of society in ancient cultures. They were valued for their ability to communicate with the gods.

→

First civilizations

By about 3500 BCE, organized societies began to emerge in various parts of the world. In ancient Mesopotamia, Egypt, India, and China, early cultures were centered around great rivers that provided water for farming, mud for making bricks, and highways for transportation. People built large cities and set up trade routes that often stretched over long distances. People in the cities depended on agricultural produce from the countryside for food.

RIVERS OF THE ANCIENT WORLD

Early societies grew up along the great rivers, on which they depended for both water and transportation. Rivers were the highways of the ancient world.

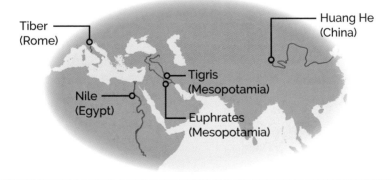

Tiber (Rome)

Huang He (China)

Tigris (Mesopotamia)

Nile (Egypt)

Euphrates (Mesopotamia)

By the 3500s BCE, the structure of these ancient societies was largely fixed. There was a small class of rulers and **nobles** who had political power. Priests were responsible for communicating with the gods and performing the correct rituals to ensure prosperity for the community. Warriors guarded the community's lands or raided the lands of its neighbors to acquire territory, animals, or slaves. Traders bought and sold goods, and officials were appointed to work for the government. In any ancient society, the majority of people were farmers or peasants responsible for producing food and other resources. Many people who worked on the land were slaves, including people who had been captured in wars. They were considered to be at the lowest level of society.

Division into classes

The class to which a family belonged was usually based on the father's job. This was the case in India, for example. By the 1500s BCE, Hindu society in India was divided into four main groups: the Brahmins, who were the priests; the Kshatriyas, or rulers, warriors, and officials; the Vaishyas, the traders and **artisans**; and the Shudras, or laborers.

POTTERY

Artisans who made pottery, furniture, tools, and clothes belonged to the class of Vaishyas in Indian society.
→

BRAHMIN

The Brahmins were the highest caste in Indian society because of their understanding of Hindu scripture and teachings. →

People outside these groups belonged to a fifth group, the Dalit, who are often called the Untouchables. Other early societies evolved a similar class structure. They later changed, however, whereas in India the system became fixed for centuries.

In India the system became known as the caste system. People born into a caste, or class, remained in it, and marriage between different castes was forbidden. The system survived until the 1900s, when Indian governments outlawed it to encourage social mobility.

IN SUMMARY

- The growth of complex societies led to more specialized roles for individuals, such as priests, warriors, traders, or craftspeople.

- The work people did was reflected in their social class.

- In India, class roles became fixed in a caste system.

SOCIAL CLASSES

The division of society into classes began thousands of years ago. The classes have varied at different times and in different places.

When societies emerged in ancient Greece in around the 800s BCE, society was divided into two broad groups: free men and slaves. Slaves had no legal rights and were the property of the free men. By the 400s BCE, when Athens was the most important **city-state** in Greece, social classes had become more complicated.

SLAVES

This Roman carving shows a prisoner of war with a rope around his neck. He most likely became a slave.

Free men were divided into metics, who were foreign-born men who moved to Athens to work, and **citizens**. To be a citizen, a man had to be born of Athenian parents. Unlike citizens, metics had to pay taxes and sometimes serve in the army. They could not own property or land. Women and children had no rights and were not included in the Greek social order.

Ancient Rome

In the 100s BCE, the Romans of Italy became the dominant power in the Mediterranean region. Their society was very hierarchical. Everyone was ranked in order, from leaders at the top to slaves at the bottom. The class system also became more complicated. Romans were divided into citizens and non-citizens but also into slaves and non-slaves. Citizens were divided into a small group of nobles called the patricians. The other citizens were known as the plebians or plebs. The patricians had more rights and political power than the plebs.

TIMELINE

400s BCE In ancient Athens, free men are divided into citizens and metics depending on their place of birth.

100s BCE Roman society is divided between the aristocracy, known as the patricians, and ordinary citizens, known as the plebians, or plebs.

ca. 700 CE A **feudal society** emerges in Europe, based on the control of land and the importance of nobles and **knights** in the frequent wars of the period.

The system seemed to be unfair to the plebs, but the Romans told a story to explain why it was good for the whole of society. In the story, a body resented its head for doing no work. The head stopped passing food to the body, so the body became weak. In the story the head represented the patricians and the body was the plebs. The two relied on each other—just as the plebs and the patricians had to rely on each other.

From the 400s to the 200s BCE, however, the plebs gained more power thanks to political reforms in Rome. The patricians became less influential. Although the patricians remained the social **elite**, plebians now became the ruling elite.

A feudal system

The Roman Empire in the West fell in 476 CE. In the period that followed, warlords in Europe fought for territory. Some eventually came to rule large regions as kings. They were supported by powerful nobles called barons, who provided armies to fight on behalf of the kings.

WOMEN

This carving from ancient Rome shows an emperor (*center*) surrounded by the patricians who dominated politics in the early Roman Empire.

↓

KNIGHTS

In the Middle Ages, rulers relied on mounted soldiers called knights to fight their wars. This made the knights important members of European society.

In northern Europe a new hierarchical social order emerged in the 700s, called the feudal system. Kings gave land to barons, and in exchange the barons had to fulfill certain duties, including raising armies in times of war. The barons raised armies of mounted soldiers, called knights, to serve the king. As payment, the barons gave parts of their land to knights. Knights lived in manor houses on large estates. They rented out their land to farmers or allowed peasants to use it in return for a share of their harvest.

ENGLISH SOCIETY IN THE 1000s

The *Domesday Book* of 1086 divided English society into classes based on a hierarchical feudal system. Few people owned land.

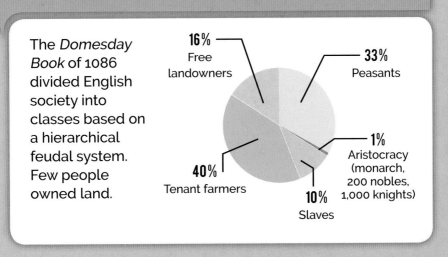

16% Free landowners

33% Peasants

1% Aristocracy (monarch, 200 nobles, 1,000 knights)

40% Tenant farmers

10% Slaves

Under the feudal system, society was shaped like a pyramid. The king and a few senior barons were at the top and a larger group of less important nobles, knights, and independent farmers called sokemen or squires were in the middle. At the bottom of the pyramid, the vast majority of society was made up of tenant farmers called villeins, peasants, and slaves.

Rising challenges

By the 1300s, feudal society started to decline. New weapons such as the longbow had made knights less important on the battlefield. Arrows fired by longbows could pierce any armor worn by knights. The feudal social system based on keeping knights ready to fight consequently became less important.

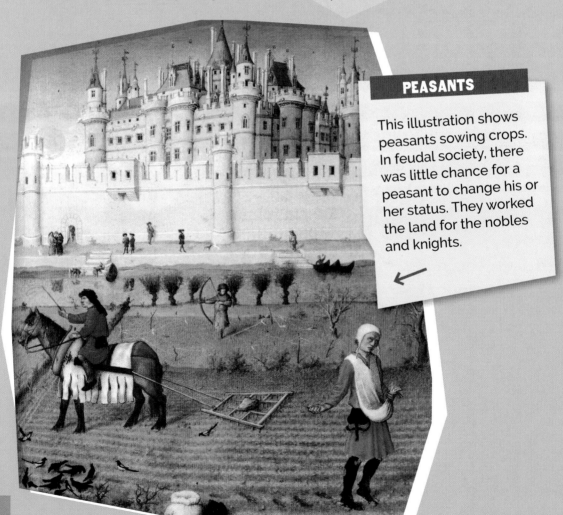

PEASANTS

This illustration shows peasants sowing crops. In feudal society, there was little chance for a peasant to change his or her status. They worked the land for the nobles and knights.

CARAVAN

Feudal society was weakened by the rise of trade and the growing use of money. Merchants brought goods to Europe from as far away as Asia.

Another challenge to feudal society came from the changing economy. Money had become more important for buying and selling goods. Instead of carrying out duties for their lords, nobles started to pay them money. Peasants left the land and moved to towns and cities to work for wages.

At the same time, a new merchant class emerged in Europe's towns and cities. They made their living from buying and selling goods. They traveled long distances to find luxuries to sell at home. These merchants would become the basis of a large middle class—and they would dominate society in Europe and its colonies for centuries to come.

IN SUMMARY

■ In ancient Greece and Rome, political power was closely associated with the idea of citizenship.

■ A feudal system emerged in Europe to support a society based on warfare and the control of land.

■ The rise of trade weakened the ties of feudal society.

TRADE AND INDUSTRY

Since ancient times it has been easy to tell who is rich or poor. Knowing why some people are rich and some are poor has always been more difficult.

Even after the decline of feudal society, the lives of medieval Europeans were still dominated by class structure. Society was now considered to be divided into three "estates." The third and lowest estate was made up of the commoners: peasants, craftsmen, and merchants.

APPRENTICE

By the Middle Ages, artisans such as this baker closely guarded their skills and passed them on by training their own **apprentices**. →

The second estate was the nobility, who had many privileges, but also obligations, such as protecting the commoners who lived on their land. The first estate was the educated clergy. The church offered commoners a way to improve their place in the social order by educating them and allowing them to rise through the ranks of the clergy.

In the 1300s, this system began to change. Some commoners grew wealthy, which gave them social status. Schools and universities appeared across Europe, making education accessible by more people. The nobility began to marry wealthy commoners, and commoners even served at royal courts, which had previously been positions open only to nobles.

Unlike in feudal society, peasants were legally free. Some peasants made enough money from selling the food they grew to buy land and employ their own workers.

TIMELINE

1400s — Merchants invest in large-scale exploration to find goods to trade from around the globe.

ca.1750 — The steam engine becomes the basis of the Industrial Revolution, which leads to increased **mechanization** of labor and a concentration of workers in cities.

1848 — Karl Marx writes *The Communist Manifesto*, declaring that workers should revolt to overthrow the capitalists who are oppressing them.

They earned a profit on their goods. Some peasants paid for an education for their sons, who became apprentices, priests, or lawyers. Peasants could now escape the social position in which they were born.

The birth of capitalism

The most mobile social group were the merchants and bankers. They often started from humble beginnings, but became very wealthy. From the 1400s, European merchants started to travel the world, looking for unusual goods to bring back to Europe and sell for a profit. They used new ships that had been developed to sail across open oceans. They paid for their voyages by borrowing money from bankers, then repaying the loan after their voyage. European sailors found new sea routes to Asia. At the same time, Europeans reached the Americas, and began to settle there.

BANKING

Modern banking began in the towns of northern Italy during the Renaissance. It soon spread across Europe. ↓

CARAVEL

Portuguese shipbuilders developed the caravel. It was sturdy enough to sail in rough seas and had a large hold to carry cargo.

←

The growth of international trade changed society from the 1700s. It led to the growth of what became known as **capitalism**. The change was made possible by an agricultural revolution that had taken place in the middle of the 1700s. The use of new mechanized farming equipment led to the final collapse of the feudal system.

GROWTH OF THE WORLD ECONOMY

The emergence of capitalism and the later Industrial Revolution led to rapid industrial growth. These estimates give the total of gross world product in the equivalent of billions of dollars.

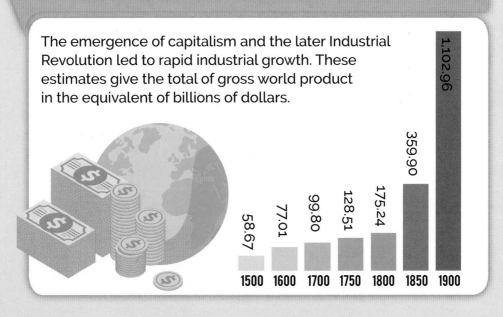

1500	1600	1700	1750	1800	1850	1900
58.67	77.01	99.80	128.51	175.24	359.90	1,102.96

The change in society had two consequences. The availability of more food led to an increase in the global population, and with fewer laborers needed to work in the fields, more people lived in cities and towns.

The Industrial Revolution

By the late 1700s, the social changes were magnified by changes in industry that began in Great Britain. The invention of the steam engine led to the invention of machines that did work previously done by people. Machines meant that a wide range of goods could be made more quickly and cheaply than ever before. Factories were built to house the machines. People flocked to the cities to work in the factories. Wages were low and many workers lived in poverty. Poor sanitation, dirty water, and cramped living quarters became normal for millions of urban working people across Europe and America.

CHILD LABOR

Children as young as six were sent to work in factories or mines. They earned money for their families, but missed out on education and many parts of a full childhood. →

Economic relationships

The poor living conditions of the industrial working class led to a new theory of society. In a series of books published in the mid-1800s, Karl Marx and his friend, Friedrich Engels, described society as being defined by its economic relationships. In place of the old class system based on the nobility, gentry, and peasantry, these men identified a system based on workers and employers. Employers were the capitalists who owned the factories, and workers were the poor **proletariat**.

TRANSPORTATION

The advent of the railroad in the 1830s, followed by the invention of the bicycle in the 1870s, made it easier for people to travel and meet people outside their own communities.

IN SUMMARY

■ Capitalism and the Industrial Revolution increasingly divided society between people who owned businesses and people who were workers.

■ The Industrial Revolution resulted in millions of workers living in small homes in overcrowded cities.

THEORIES OF SOCIAL ORGANIZATION

Karl Marx was not the first person to wonder about the nature of society. Thinkers had questioned how people lived together for centuries.

Most ancient cultures had myths and legends that explained how their society was created and how it was organized. In ancient Rome, the legendary story of Romulus and Remus explained the founding of the city. A female wolf saved the brothers from drowning.

SHE-WOLF

According to Roman myth, Romulus and Remus were saved from drowning by a she-wolf who fed them in a cave. Romulus went on to found the city of Rome. →

Romulus killed Remus in a fight before going on to found Rome. For most Romans, the division of society into patricians and plebians had originated with the founding of Rome itself and was not something to be questioned.

Backed by religion

In the Middle Ages, the feudal system that dominated Europe was backed by the teachings of the Catholic Church. Kings claimed that their authority came from God and that God had assigned all individuals to their appropriate status in society.

The first theories of social organization were developed in Italy in the 1500s, during the cultural movement known as the Renaissance. Thinkers began to reject traditional ideas based on church teaching in favor of ideas based on the importance of human rather than divine influence.

TIMELINE

1513   Niccolò Machiavelli writes *The Prince*, describing for the first time a ruler's duties to his subjects.

1762   In *The Social Contract*, Jean-Jacques Rousseau proposes the idea that a society is based on an unspoken agreement between rulers and their subjects.

1789   Rousseau's ideas contribute to the outbreak of the French Revolution, which overthrows the French monarchy.

Also in the 1500s, the growth of towns and the emergence of capitalism changed Italy's economy. This added to the new spirit of individualism. People saw the society in which they lived as something created by humans, not by God.

Machiavelli and *The Prince*

Niccolò Machiavelli was an Italian philosopher, historian, and politician in the 1500s. Like other thinkers of the time, he questioned the power of the Catholic Church over people's lives.

In 1513, Machiavelli wrote *The Prince* (it was published in 1532, after his death). Machiavelli argued that a ruler should look after the welfare of his subjects. To do so, the ruler could act in an immoral way if necessary. Machiavelli's argument was influential at a time when people were thinking about how to free society from the control of the Catholic Church.

MACHIAVELLI

Machiavelli was one of the first people to suggest that rulers had a duty to take care of the societies they ruled, even by making unpopular decisions or acting in a cruel way.

←

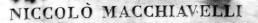

NICCOLÒ MACCHIAVELLI

The Enlightenment

In the 1700s, during a period called the Enlightenment, some thinkers created a new intellectual way of seeing the world. They used reason and logic to think about government and society. At the heart of this new way of thinking was the French writer Jean-Jacques Rousseau. His ideas would help inspire the French Revolution of 1789.

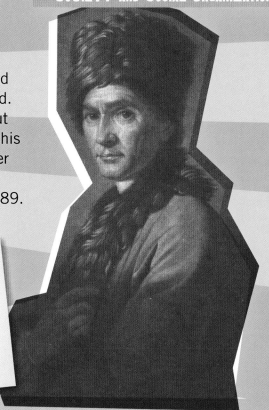

ROUSSEAU

Jean-Jacques Rousseau suggested that citizens had responsibilities to their society. Such ideas were the basis of the Enlightenment, a period when thinkers tried to apply reason to understanding the world.

REMAINING COMMUNIST COUNTRIES

Communism was a theory of social organization that began in the 1840s. It became widespread in the first half of the 1900s. By 2017, only five communist countries remained.

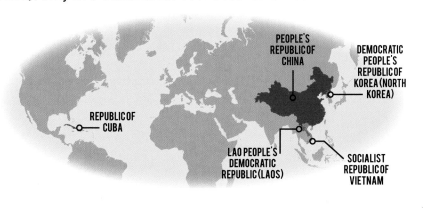

PEOPLE'S REPUBLIC OF CHINA

DEMOCRATIC PEOPLE'S REPUBLIC OF KOREA (NORTH KOREA)

REPUBLIC OF CUBA

LAO PEOPLE'S DEMOCRATIC REPUBLIC (LAOS)

SOCIALIST REPUBLIC OF VIETNAM

The French Revolution

In 1762, Rousseau wrote *The Social Contract*. It opened with the words, "Man is born free, and everywhere he is in chains." Rousseau argued that rulers and their subjects had a responsibility to behave in a certain way. He called this the "social contract." Like Machiavelli, Rousseau argued that rulers had a duty to look after their subjects. But he went further, saying that if a ruler did not fulfill this obligation, the people had the right to get rid of him or her. Another French philosopher, Charles Louis de Secondat, known as Montesquieu, proposed that the monarch's power should be limited by parliament and the **judiciary**. Such works transformed the way people thought about society. In the late 1700s, such ideas were the basis of revolutions in North America and France. The people who made up society wanted to be able to govern themselves, not to be ruled by monarchs.

REVOLUTION

In 1789, the French people overthrew the monarchy. The king and queen were executed in 1793.

Marxism

The mid-1700s saw the start of the Industrial Revolution. Workers toiled in factories and mines, while a new middle class emerged. They owned and managed factories and stores. The land-owning aristocracy found its social status threatened by the importance of the new industrialists.

These social changes lay behind the thinking of Karl Marx. In *The Communist Manifesto* of 1848, Marx divided society into workers and employers, the capitalists. He believed that society had lost its traditional unity. It was now based on one class exploiting the other. Marx called for a revolution in which the workers of the world would overthrow their employers. At the time, the book had little impact. By the mid-1900s, communism would form the basis for governments around the world.

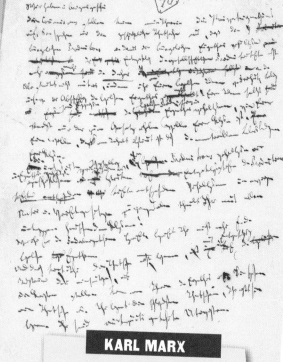

KARL MARX

In *The Communist Manifesto*, Karl Marx argued that society was divided because the interests of the capitalists and the workers were not the same.

IN SUMMARY

■ Renaissance and Enlightenment thinkers began to question the traditional organization of society and the responsibilities of a ruler.

■ Industrialization led to the emergence of communism, which suggested that property should belong not to individuals but to society as a whole.

THE INDIVIDUAL AND SOCIETY

The question of whether the needs of individuals or the needs of society are more important is still debated. People hold different views on the subject.

When the Founding Fathers signed the US Constitution in 1787, they laid down the principles of how the United States would be governed. As well as defining how the political and legal systems would work, the Constitution defined the rights of citizens. Every American had the right to life, liberty, property, and the pursuit of happiness.

CONSTITUTION

The US Constitution (1787) and the Bill of Rights (1791) defined the rights of citizens in the United States. →

Setting out the rights of citizens in a legally binding document created a precedent for each person to be treated as an individual rather than simply as a member of society. This idea was called individualism. It had its roots in the ideas of the European Renaissance.

A similar process took place during the French Revolution. The revolutionaries emphasized the rights of people as individuals. Throughout the 1800s, the growth of education, the emergence of widely available newspapers and magazines, and the extension of the right to vote to virtually all adult males encouraged individual opportunity. In industrialized economies, the idea of a person's potential being defined by his or her class grew weaker—although it never vanished completely.

Social rules

Despite the rise of individualism, society remained important in shaping people's lives. In the 1800s, people who broke society's rules of acceptable behavior were subject to exclusion from "polite society."

TIMELINE

1787 The US Constitution outlines the rights of citizens, but fails to include women, African Americans, and Native Americans.

1933 Adolf Hitler becomes chancellor of Germany, leading to the creation of a **militaristic** society in which the individual has few rights.

ca. 2015 The Millennials—people born around 2000—become young adults. They are widely criticized for feeling entitled to social and economic success.

A fear of social disapproval helped to ensure that people generally behaved in an acceptable way. This situation was reflected in the popularity of books about manners in the late 1800s and early 1900s. These books explained to people how to behave "correctly" in society, from rules on how to greet members of the aristocracy to details of which spoon or fork to use for which course of a meal.

Dictators and society

A challenge to individualism emerged in the mid-1900s with the growth of political extremism. Communism and **fascism** both created a social system in which individuals were far less important than society as a whole. Dictators such as Joseph Stalin in the Soviet Union, Adolf Hitler in Germany, Mao Zedong in China, and Pol Pot in Cambodia forced millions of people to observe their ideas of a uniform, militaristic society. People who disagreed with the system were persecuted, imprisoned, or killed.

NAZI RALLY

In Germany in the 1930s, Adolf Hitler tried to create a militaristic society in which the rights of individuals were largely nonexistent.

←

Neighbors spied on each other, and children were encouraged to report the behavior of their parents.

In the Soviet Union, China, and Cambodia, millions of people died. In Germany, Hitler's fascist beliefs led to World War II (1939–1945) and the genocide of millions of Jews and other people in the Holocaust.

Society and welfare

Families had traditionally looked after their own members. The mass poverty that had followed the Industrial Revolution in the 1800s convinced many people that society as a whole had a responsibility to help its less fortunate members.

POSTWAR

The late 1940s and 1950s are often seen as a golden age. Jobs were widely available and there was a rise in the birth rate after World War II. ↑

SHRINKING FAMILY SIZES

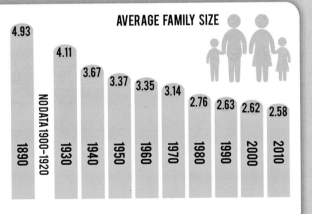

The size of the average American family has been shrinking for over 100 years. Improved birth control and changing attitudes toward families mean that couples have fewer children.

AVERAGE FAMILY SIZE

Year	Size
1890	4.93
NO DATA 1900–1920	
1930	4.11
1940	3.67
1950	3.37
1960	3.35
1970	3.14
1980	2.76
1990	2.63
2000	2.62
2010	2.58

By the early 1900s, this view had led to the gradual creation of systems known as "social security." These tax-funded systems provide people in need with health and pension benefits. Social security systems are now universal in the West, but they remain the subject of much political debate. Some people do not believe that society should support those who have little because they say that prevents individuals from trying to find a job and improve their own lives. Other people argue that taking money from people through taxation is also wrong. It was a similar argument to this that Britain's prime minister Margaret Thatcher made when she claimed that "there is no such thing as society."

Rise of individualism

By the beginning of the 2000s, balance had been established between individualism and society. The shift from manual and factory jobs to office jobs, a rising level of education, and the smaller size of the average family all encouraged a rise in individualism.

NEW THREAT

Radical Muslims see the individualism of Western democracy as being anti-Islamic. They argue that people should all be subject to strict laws.

CLASSROOM

Will children who are at school today grow up in a society that supports them in times of need, or will they have to rely on themselves and their families?

For some people, however, individualism has become too dominant. They describe the generations since World War II as the "me, me, me" society. Millennials—people who became adults in the decade after 2000—are often criticized for feeling entitled to a certain level of comfort. Critics say they are putting their own needs ahead of those of society. It seems certain that debates about whether individuals or society are more important will continue.

IN SUMMARY

■ The rise of democracy in the 1800s led to a more inclusive version of society.

■ After World War I (1914–1918), dictatorial rulers tried to remove individualism from society.

■ Individualism made a return at the end of the 1900s.

THE WORLD TODAY

Modern societies vary widely in the freedom they give to their individual members and in the support individuals receive from society.

SCANDINAVIA The Scandinavian countries follow what is called the Nordic Model to balance free-market capitalism with highly developed welfare states.

North America

FRANCE In 2016, France was one of three states to spend more than 30 percent of its GDP on social welfare. The others were Denmark and Finland.

30%

Europe

UNITED STATES In the early 2000s, the richest 20 percent of Americans owned 85 percent of national wealth.

85%

Africa

WELFARE STATES

In welfare states, governments pass direct or indirect benefits on to members of society who need financial support. Typical benefits include free education, free health care, and pensions for the elderly. There are numerous models of welfare states, in which individuals make greater or lesser finanical contributions to the system.

South America

GREAT SOCIETY

In the mid-1960s, US president Lyndon B. Johnson launched a program he called the Great Society. He wanted to improve the government's provision of education, medical care, and transportation, while coping with urban problems and rural poverty. Johnson's ideas shaped US politics until the 1980s, when many critics complained that the government was too involved in the lives of ordinary Americans.

FACTFILE:
NATIONS WITH SIGNIFICANT POPULATIONS OF **HUNTER-GATHERERS** IN 2016:

Andaman Islands
Brazil
Central African Republic
Colombia
Democratic Republic of the Congo
Malaysia
Philippines
Tanzania
Thailand
Venezuela

FACTFILE:
Five countries had communist societies in 2017:

China
Cuba
Laos
North Korea
Vietnam

FACTFILE:
In 2017, six societies were matriarchies:

Akan (Ghana)
Bribri (Costa Rica)
Garo (India)
Minangkabau (Indonesia)
Mosuo (China)
Nagovisi (New Guinea)

ISRAEL Israel was home to the kibbutz movement in which members lived and worked in a communal agricultural settlement. Today, Israel still has 74 communal kibbutzim.

Asia

NORTH KOREA North Korea is ruled by the communist dictator Kim Jong-un. The Communist Party discourages displays of individualism in a strictly controlled society.

INDIA Hindu families in India commonly follow a model in which generations of a family share the same home, which is under the control of a patriarch.

43

TIMELINE

ca. 30,000 BCE — Early humans begin to paint the walls of caves with images of animals, people, and the shapes of their own hands.

ca. 8000 BCE — Humans begin to learn to grow crops, which gradually leads to the emergence of settled communities.

ca. 7500 BCE — Catal Huyuk is settled in what is now Anatolia. It is the oldest known settlement in the world. It was made possible by advances in agriculture during the Neolithic Revolution.

ca. 3500 BCE — Complex civilizations develop around the world, with large cities, extensive trade, social hierarchies, and wide differences between the rich and the poor.

ca. 1500 BCE — A caste system begins to emerge when a people known as the Aryans arrived in what is now India.

400s BCE — In ancient Athens, free men were divided into citizens and metics depending on where they were born.

100s BCE — Roman society is divided between the aristocracy, known as the patricians, and ordinary people, known as the plebians, or plebs.

ca. 700 CE — A feudal system emerges in Europe, based on the control of land and the importance of nobles and knights in the frequent wars of the period.

ca. 1250 — The Renaissance begins in Italy. The cultural movement is based on the ideas of ancient Greece and Rome.

1300s — Feudal society declines after mounted knights become less important in warfare. The rise of trade and a money-based economy also weakens people's dependence on the land.

1400s — Merchants invest in large-scale exploration to find goods to trade from around the globe.

1513 — Niccolò Machiavelli writes *The Prince*, describing for the first time a ruler's duties to his subjects.

ca.1750	The steam engine becomes the basis of the Industrial Revolution, which leads to increased mechanization of labor and a concentration of workers in cities.
1762	In *The Social Contract*, Jean-Jacques Rousseau proposes the idea that a society is based on an agreement between rulers and their people that can be overthrown if it functions poorly.
1776	Colonial Americans declare their independence and create the United States. The American Revolution encourages other challenges to traditional dynastic society in Europe.
1787	The US Constitution outlines the rights of citizens, but fails to include women, African Americans, and Native Americans.
1789	Ideas such as those of Rousseau contribute to the outbreak of the French Revolution, which overthrows the French monarchy.
1848	Karl Marx writes *The Communist Manifesto*, declaring that workers should revolt to overthrow the capitalists who are oppressing them.
1933	Adolf Hitler becomes chancellor of Germany, leading to the creation of a militaristic society in which the individual has few rights.
1987	British prime minister Margaret Thatcher declares in an interview, "there is no such thing as society."
ca.2015	Millennials—people born around 2000—become young adults. They are widely criticized for feeling entitled to social and economic success.

GLOSSARY

antisocial Someone who rejects the rules and customs of society.

apprentices People learning a trade from a skilled employer.

archaeological Related to the study of the past through objects and ruins.

artisans Skilled workers who make things with their hands.

barter A system in which goods are exchanged for other goods without using money.

capitalism An economic system in which individuals invest in trade and industry for profit.

caste system A system in which a person's position in society is set by birth.

citizens Legally recognized subjects of a nation–state or country.

city-state A state formed by a city and its surrounding territory.

classes Groups in society based on people's economic or social status.

concept An abstract idea.

domesticated Describes animals that have been bred to live closely with humans.

elite A select group with a superior status to the rest of society.

fascism An authoritarian, nationalistic, and militaristic system of government.

feudal society A hierarchical society based on the distribution of land.

hierarchies Societies in which members are ranked by their relative status.

hunter-gatherers People who get food by hunting, fishing, or foraging, rather than by farming.

interactions Occasions when two or more people communicate with or react to one another.

judiciary The judges and court system of a country.

knights Soldiers who fight on horseback.

mechanization Using machinery to do jobs previously done by hand.

militaristic Describes a society organized to support the armed forces.

Neolithic The New Stone Age, a period from about the 10,000s BCE to about 2000 BCE.

nobles Members of the aristocracy who traditionally held political power.

proletariat The working class in an industrial society.

radical Holding extreme views.

surplus Something left over after the required amount has been taken.

FURTHER RESOURCES

Books

Cates, David. *Karl Marx: Philosopher and Revolutionary.* Essential Lives. Edina, MN: Abdo Publishing Company, 2011.

Nardo, Don. *The Industrial Revolution's Workers and their Lives.* Library of Historical Eras. Detroit: Lucent Books, 2009.

Pulditor, Seth. *Fascism.* Major Forms of World Government. Broomall, PA: Mason Crest Publishing, 2012.

Sonneborn, Liz. *The Romans: Life in Ancient Rome.* Life in Ancient Civilizations. Minneapolis: Millbrook Press, 2009.

Stuckey, Rachel. *Your Guide to Medieval Society.* Destination Middle Ages. New York: Crabtree Publishing Company, 2010.

Websites

http://ancienthistory.mrdonn.org/
This page from Mr. Donn has details about the earliest societies on earth.

http://www.bbc.co.uk/bitesize/ks3/history/middle_ages/feudal_system_domesday_book/revision/3/
This BBC page has information about feudal society in the Middle Ages and the information gathered in the *Domesday Book*.

http://www.ducksters.com/money/capitalism.php
The Ducksters website provides an explanation of how capitalism works.

http://www.philosophyslam.org/rousseau.html
This page from Kids Philosophy Slam describes the ideas and influence of Jean-Jacques Rousseau.

http://www.socialstudiesforkids.com/subjects/enlightenment.htm
Social Studies for Kids features a collection of links to many pages about aspects of the Age of the Enlightenment.

Publisher's note to educators and parents: Our editors have carefully reviewed these websites to ensure that they are suitable for students. Many websites change frequently, however, and we cannot guarantee that a site's future contents will continue to meet our high standards of quality and educational value. Be advised that students should be closely supervised whenever they access the Internet.

INDEX